Come back—
you've missed
a few things!
merry Xmas—
Chris

2007

CHICAGO

IN PHOTOGRAPHS

CHICAGO

IN PHOTOGRAPHS

In collaboration with the travel experts at Fodor's

Thomas J. O'Gorman

GRAMERCY BOOKS
NEW YORK

© 2005 PRC Publishing,
The Chrysalis Building,
Bramley Road, London W10 6SP

An imprint of **Chrysalis** Books Group plc

Published by Gramercy Books,
an imprint of Random House Value Publishing,
a division of Random House, Inc., New York,
by arrangement with Chrysalis Books, London.

Random House
New York • Toronto • London • Sydney • Auckland
www.randomhouse.com

Printed and bound in China

A catalog record for this title is available from the Library
of Congress.

ISBN 0-517-22658-8

10 9 8 7 6 5 4 3 2 1

Credits
Editor: Anne McDowall
Designer: John Heritage
Picture Researcher: Carla Penagos
Production: Kate Rogers
Reproduction: Anorax Imaging Ltd

Dedication
For Rose Marie O'Neall, a real Chicago treasure

Additional captions
Page 1: The Chicago Theater on State Street (page 23)
Page 2: The peristyle of Ionic columns of Halsted Street (page 64)

Picture Acknowledgments

L=Left R=Right C=Center T=Top B= Bottom

© Chrysalis Image Library/Simon Clay 19, 23, 27, 34, 35, 37, 39B, 42,
48, 49, 50, 54, 58, 59, 67T, 68, 118, 120

© Churchill & Klehr Photography 2, 13, 29TR, 29BR, 31B, 33, 38,
43T, 43B, 51B, 52-53, 55T, 55B, 56B, 57, 61T, 65, 66, 67B, 69, 70T,
70B, 71, 72, 75, 76, 77, 78B, 79, 80B, 81, 83, 86L, 86-87, 88-89, 90,
91, 92B, 93, 94, 95T, 98, 99T, 100, 102, 103TR, 103BR, 105, 107T,
107B, 108T, 108B, 109, 112, 113B, 114T, 114B, 115, 116, 117, 119T,
119B, 122-123, 124, 125T, 125B

Corbis   © Alen MacWeeney/CORBIS 30, © Ralf-Finn
Hestoft/CORBIS 32, © Kevin Fleming/CORBIS 51T, © Robert
Holmes/CORBIS 60 and 113T, © ART on FILE/CORBIS 84B, ©
MAPS.com/CORBIS 128

© Dawn M Photography / Chicago Uncommon 17, 18T, 18B, 45,
80T, 84T, 85, 92T, 95B, 121

© Lonely Planet Images/Raymond Hillstrom 73, © Lonely Planet
Images/Tom Given 78T

© Photolibrary.com 7, 8, 10, 12, 14-15, 20-21, 22, 24-25, 25R, 26,
28, 31T, 36, 39T, 40-41, 44, 47, 48, 56T, 61B, 62-63, 96-97, 99B,
101, 106, 110-111

Contents

INTRODUCTION

Chicago is a city that cut its teeth on beefsteak, beer, baseball, and a unique expression of American politics. Each has shaped the contours of local culture and tastes. So too have the waterways that converge on its doorstep: Lake Michigan and the Chicago River. Their flow has connected Chicago to the waterways of the rest of the continent, imbuing it with economic power and commercial success, as well as America's finest drinking water.

Chicago just might be the country's most American city, set as it is in the center of the United States. Over a period of little more than a century and a half, it has been the nation's hub for water, rail, and air traffic. This centrality has made Chicago the capitol of the American heartland. And this is no idle boast: a quick glance displays a panorama of strength and beauty in epic proportions—both natural and man made—spread all about its crisp urban landscape. The sheer size of Lake Michigan, a great American inland sea, and the robust expanse of Chicago's architectural skyline almost overwhelm the viewer.

Chicago's geography has been its making as a great metropolis. However, its rich and diverse history have much to do with the shape and culture of the city today. It's origins—and its unusual name—go back to the native peoples who populated the region long before the French, British, or Americans staked a claim to its flatland. "Chi-gaw-goo," locals delight in announcing with a laugh, is Indian for "bad smell." It might be more accurately translated as "strong smell," a name identifying the expansive fields of small prairie onions that grew there in abundance in primeval days.

Real Chicagoans can immediately identify fellow natives merely by the manner in which they pronounce the city's name. Locals say something that sounds like "Sha-CAW-go," while all others— visitors, foreigners, and local television reporters—say "Sha-CAH-go." The city rightfully claims its own American regional dialect (the Chicago "A") and resi-dents can spot someone from outside the zip code as soon as they hear the city's name.

French explorers, including the Jesuit Father Pierre Marquette, visited Chicago in 1673. The Chevalier Robert Sur LaSalle also came to the area, while it was still in under French rule, when searching for the Mississippi. The Chevalier McCarthy, the first of many Irishmen to come to Chicago, accompanied LaSalle, and today the city's financial district is located on a street named in honor of LaSalle. Jean Pointe du Sable, a Haitian-African, was the area's first settler in the years before the American Revolution. (Today the Wrigley Building stands on the riverbank on the spot that was once his farm.)

When America was but an infant republic, the land grid of Chicago stood as the farthest outlying point in the nation's defense system, a network of forts that Thomas Jefferson's government built to strengthen security. Fort Dearborn, named for the nation's then Secretary of Defense, John Dearborn, became the fur-trading outpost's first public works project here in 1803, when Captain John Whistler, the Dublin-born grandfather of the American expatriate painter James McNeill Whistler, constructed the stockade fort. He became its first commander. Standing along the high palisades of the Chicago River, on what today is the corner of Wacker Drive and Michigan Avenue, the fort became ground zero for Chicago's urban settlement. During the War of 1812, Native Americans in the service of the British led an attack on the residents of the fort who were attempting to escape to Fort Detroit. Their massacre and the burning of the fort are among Chicago's first

▶ **Chicago River:** *Chicago's riverscape looking west to the flatland of the prairie. At mid-view the Chicago River forks north and south. The riverbank on the right contains the earliest civilian settlement from fur-trading days, when Mark Beaubien's tavern was the heart of town life. The many bridges spanning the water open to permit commercial and private vessels to pass.*

great historic events of note. So too was the rebuilding of the fort, setting a pattern for Chicago resilience in the future.

By American standards, Chicago is a late bloomer: Boston and New York were almost 200 years old by the time Chicago was founded as a town in 1833, and then as a city, in 1837. Illinois itself had only been a state for less than 20 years at that date. Chicago counted only 4000 residents at the start of its journey to urban greatness. But its potential was unleashed by its own hunger for success. Only months after Chicago received its official charter, the city's leaders made plans to finance the most important project in Chicago's history—the Illinois and Michigan Canal. Begun in 1838 and completed ten years later, the canal was a waterway joining Lake Michigan with the Illinois River 90 miles away. When

completed, the canal ultimately connected Chicago to the Gulf of Mexico, via New Orleans, by way of the Mississippi, and assured the city of a viable economic future. All the waterways of the nation were then linked through one central spot on the map—Chicago. From that moment on, the city became the nation's commercial hub. Goods and farm products from the interior of the nation easily found their way to Chicago. The canal was also the catalyst for the immigration of the Irish, whose influence on the political, cultural, educational, and religious life of Chicago is without equal. There the Irish found themselves at the center of great opportunities, both commercial and political.

Chicago's geographical centrality influenced many entrepreneurs. It was no accident that when Cyrus McCormick, the inventor of the reaper, a machine

that changed the way the world farmed, sought a place to build his production factory, he selected Chicago as the ideal site. His business later grew to become the International Harvester Corporation, and the McCormick family exercised a huge influence on Chicago philanthropy and culture.

Today Chicago can boast one of the world's busiest and most successful commodity exchanges—the Chicago Board of Trade and the Chicago Mercantile Exchange. Their origins were an outgrowth of the canal traffic that brought enormous quantities of grain and agricultural commodities to the city, as they were shipped through the commercial gateway of America, creating vast fortunes in the process.

On the heels of the canal's completion, the Galena and Chicago Union Railroad began. It set in motion what was to become Chicago's greatest claim to fame—its reputation as the railroad center of America. Thanks to the efforts of Chicago's man in Washington, Illinois Senator Stephen A. Douglas—who ran against Abraham Lincoln in 1860 for the presidency—Chicago received lucrative federal assistance in the effort to converge all of America's railway lines within the city limits. Chicago ultimately became the terminus for all rail travel across the country, the Illinois Central Station was the largest rail terminal in the world when it opened in 1860.

Over the course of the next century Chicago expanded on the back of America's rail industry. George Pullman developed and produced his sleeping car empire in Chicago. The city also hosted its first national presidential convention in 1860, as Republicans came and nominated Abraham Lincoln. The city went on to host 24 more presidential conventions between 1860 and 1996. Chicago was an easy city to travel to and visitors were well accommodated during their stay. Among those who helped to ensure the availability of suitable accommodations was hotelier Potter Palmer, a titan of Chicago commerce.

◀ **State Street:** *There is no more recognizable signage in Chicago than the great clock at Marshall Field & Company or the distinctive neon of the Chicago Theater. Each is a historic part of the life of State Street, the traditional downtown commercial strip. State Street is also the numerical dividing line between east and west in the city's urban grid.*

The character of Chicago was further defined by the presence of the Chicago Stockyards, an industry employing thousands of hardworking immigrants and locally born Americans after it opened in 1865. The thriving livestock industry went on to make enormous fortunes for Chicagoans such as Philip Danforth Armour, Gustavus Swift, Nelson Morris, and Patrick Cudahy. These meatpackers invented and patented the process for the large-scale slaughtering, dressing, and delivery of meat products across the nation and around the world via refrigerated rail cars. The economic trickle-down further boosted Chicago's run-away economy and power.

When the immigration boom hit America in the 1880s, Chicago became an attractive destination for millions of immigrants, as it provided a healthy alternative to the crowded, run-down urban centers of the east. Neighborhoods around the stockyards soon became a microcosm of European living. The expansive development of the network of parochial schools built by the Archdiocese of Chicago became a quick passage to assimilation as younger immigrant children learned how to become American, adapting to local Chicago customs.

No event in Chicago's history, however, had more of an impact on its urban development than the Great Fire of 1871. After the warmest, driest autumn in its history, the city experienced an unprecedented series of fires that finally resulted in the out-of-control cataclysm of October 8th. Prairie winds fanned the flames to such an extent that the conflagration became unstoppable. Cyclones of heat and fire raced from 12th Street on the south to Fullerton Avenue on the north, and from Lake Michigan on the east to the south branch of the Chicago River on the west. Buildings exploded from the heat and entire blocks went up in flames. At one point the fire jumped over the Chicago River, spreading north. Only one house and the Chicago Water Tower were spared.

Three-fifths of the city center was left in ruins before rain brought an end to the fire on October 9th. But the myth of Mrs. Catherine O'Leary and her cow, which allegedly caused the disaster by kicking over a lantern, would endure. The story was only officially debunked by Chicago Alderman Edward M. Burke and the Chicago City Council more than a century and a quarter later.

As dramatic as the Great Fire was, the city recovered remarkably quickly: Chicago men of business were on trains for New York before the smoke cleared. Potter Palmer, department-store magnate Marshall Field, and a host of leading entrepreneurs, men of wealth who had lost everything, endeavored to sell Chicago and its future. The financial investment by eastern bankers in the future of Chicago became the largest financial investment in American history at the time. The scale with which Chicago was rebuilt was unprecedented in American history. It really was a phoenix rising from the ashes.

Chicago was the fastest growing city on earth in the latter half of the nineteenth century. The 4,000 citizens of its founding were quickly expanded at such speed that there were almost 300,000 residents by the time of the 1871 disaster. By 1880, there were more than half a million. That doubled again to one million by 1890, and by 1910 there were in excess of two million people calling Chicago home.

As the city was rebuilt from the ground up commercial properties rose with a new panache and splendor, touching the sky, thanks to the inventive architects who made Chicago home. William LaBarron Jenney's Home Insurance Building built in 1882, at 12 stories, is considered the first skyscraper in the world. Monuments to local financial achieve-

ments such as these were so new and exciting that soon industrial barons were placing commissions before the array of the city's finest architects—Daniel Burnham, John Wellborn Root, Louis Sullivan, Dankmar Adler, and a very young Frank Lloyd Wright.

Wright began his career in Chicago as Sullivan's protégé before he was fired for working outside the firm. He was too impatient, reinventing how American families lived through the creation of what he called his Prairie Style homes. Architects such as Wright were redesigning the city in a crisp style that seemed to reflect the simplicity and horizontal character of the flat prairie landscape. They spoke of "organic" designs and functional utility. With all the self-made fortunes in town, architects were always busy, as whole neighborhoods arose, and unique enclaves fashioned for the elite dotted the contours of the lakefront. No other city in the nation was undergoing such fast-paced redevelopment, and in the process a whole new idea of urban life was being defined.

Nothing demonstrated Chicago's urban resiliency more than the great Fair of 1893—the World's Columbian Exposition. Though it was to mark the 400th Anniversary of Columbus's voyage to the New World, for most Chicagoans it was the glorious celebration of their recovery and growth into the most modern city in America. In a marshy area of the city,

◀ **The "EL":** *Chicago's most enduring landmark the "EL," as the city's elevation network of trains is known, is fast and dependable. As the trains enter the commercial center of the city they encircle the old footprint of the nineteenth-century downtown. The "Loop" formed by the great iron trestles of the tracks has become the name Chicagoans traditionally use in referring to this part of town.*

near 55th Street and the lake, known as Jackson Park, the Fair's chief architect, Daniel Burnham, sketched plans to transform its geography into the showcase of world attention. He built "The White City," the shimmering neo-classically designed buildings of the fair. Twenty-seven million people from around the world would travel to see this spectacle. Nothing before had ever "showcased" Chicago so brilliantly as this singular event. Over the six months it was open, visitors saw displayed the modern age crashing into the last vestiges of Victorian life. Among the popular items found at the Fair, in addition to Buffalo Bill Cody's Wild West Show, was the electric light bulb, the phonograph, the telephone, the automobile, and the electric elevator. Many of these modern wonders were the product of the inventiveness of the Fair's most celebrated participant, Thomas Edison.

Outside the Jackson Park confines of the Fair, the number-one attraction was the stunning Auditorium Theater Building designed and built by Sullivan and Adler. At 18 stories, it was the tallest building in the world at the time. Most heartland Americans had never seen such a sight. The structure not only contained the finest opera house in America, it also had a luxury hotel and a commercial office building, making it one of the country's first mixed-use buildings. The fact that it was "air-conditioned" further captured people's imagination.

A lady called Mrs. Potter Palmer also startled visitors with a large collection of Impressionist paintings specifically assembled for the Fair. Their strangely blurring composition was not to everyone's tastes, but Chicago tempers flared when the Infanta of Spain, sister of the king, refused an invitation to Mrs Palmer's lakefront castle for dinner with the city's elite, on the grounds that the Princess could not dine with anyone whose husband ran a hotel. Even though the Palmers ate off dishes of pure gold, they could not persuade the Infanta. She was, however, prevailed upon to pay a visit to the Palmers' reception. Chicagoans never

forgot the slight by the foreigner. "Chicago doesn't cotton to royalty," was what one former mayor said.

The city entered the modern age before the century turned. It was proud of what it had accomplished. The "Second City," as the rebuilt Chicago was known, was modern inside and out. So many inventive, self-made personalities had come to make it their home; it was the envy of the nation.

In the twentieth century, Chicago continued its passionate yearning for the modern. The continuous refinement of its architectural style would make it the architectural capital of America. Daniel Burnham and John Wellborn Root's professional partnership had produced the Reliance Building in 1890 and transformed American architecture for all times with its steel-framed and glass construction. Their building remains the mother of all American glass-and-steel high-rise designs. Burnham would go on to create a "Plan for Chicago," in 1909, which remains the chief architectural road map for urban design in Chicago. In every era of prosperity, another element of his plan is expanded on.

Chicagoans cherish the lakefront and the 27 miles of natural parkland that frame it. Burnham called it "the city's emerald necklace." Thanks to A. Montgomery Ward, the powerful mail-order catalogue king, the lakefront remains "forever open, clear, and free." Ward used his vast financial resources in the early decades of the twentieth century to block any encroachment to the lands along the lakefront. His vigilance prohibited even a museum from being built on the public right-of-way.

Though Chicago is often known around the world for its Prohibition Era hoodlums and gangland crime headlines, the colorful characters of that period in its life also included individuals who never used a machine gun. America's first citizen Saint, the Italian immigrant Mother Frances Xavier Cabrini, worked for years in Chicago building hospitals and settlement houses for rescuing Italian newcomers who did not strike it rich. In such critical work, Chicago's other famed social pioneers, Jane Addams and Ellen Starr, started Hull House as a way of helping the vast population of uneducated immigrants who filled many of the city's neighborhoods.

In all of Chicago life, however, nothing aligns the stars more than the city's two professional baseball

teams—the Chicago White Sox (Southside) and the Chicago Cubs (Northside). For generations of Chicagoans, loyalty to one of these two major league ball clubs is a defining element of life. For many this allegiance transcends everything, including moves to other parts of the city. Families maintain those loyalties in the face of all changes, transitions, or even seasonal success.

Politics are the city's other substantive anchor. Like baseball, politics is both a team sport and a spectator sport for many. But it is truly the glue of local life. Chicago is said to be "the city that works." The axiom is still true, today more than ever. Chicagoans expect the infrastructure of everyday life to operate with efficiency and dependability. The traffic should flow, the street lights shine bright, the snow plowed, the pot

holes repaired, public transportation must be dependable, and the garbage must be collected.

Politics in Chicago is a mundane business. It is consumed with the details of everyday life. In return, Chicagoans are loyal to those who keep things well oiled and looking good. Outsiders rail about "the machine," or carp about "corruption." Most real Chicagoans know that they have America's last great urban political organization. Over the years, the source of all local political power has been the Cook County Democratic Organization. This political network is the child of generations of Chicago politicos, party leaders, many of whom served as the city's chief executives—Mayors Anton Cermak, Edward J. Kelly, Martin F. Kennelly, and Richard J. Daley. These men were not only local politicians, they also held sway on a national level. Kelly, for example, is responsible for President Franklin D. Roosevelt's seeking his unprecedented third term and for orchestrating Senator Harry S. Truman's place on the ticket for Roosevelt's fourth and fatal term that many knew he could not survive. Kelly's influence changed America, bolstered the war outcome and ensured a tough American president in the post-war years. Daley, on the other hand, is credited with helping John F. Kennedy capture the White House in 1960 by his strong leadership in Cook County. Kennedy never forgot what Daley did for him. He too, changed America through his influence.

Daley's more than 20 years in office transformed Chicago, expanded its stability, and fashioned it into one of America's most livable cities. He is unfairly blamed for issues he neither created, nor could resolve in his time in office, such as Federal Public Housing, the poor choices made by his Democratic Party in 1968 and his defense of the city's safety during the 1968 Democratic National Convention. Daley made it possible for Chicago to survive as a city long after others sang its requiem. The city's present day viability is built upon his achievements. He championed the construction of the University of Illinois, but dislodged thousands of Italian and Greek residents on Chicago's Westside in the process. That said, the university is among the most successful urban campuses in America and attracts unprecedented numbers of students. It was his dream to provide the

◀ **View over Lincoln Park:** *On the flat prairie, Chicago built its own mountain range of incomparable American architecture. This view looks south, over the canopies of trees in Lincoln Park, named in honor of Illinois' favorite son, Abraham Lincoln. The buildings just beyond the trees are stately co-ops on "the Gold Coast," the elite enclave off Lake Shore Drive. The John Hancock Building with its distinctive black X design towers above it all.*

▼ **"The Four Seasons":** *The mosaic wall cataloguing Chicago's curious climatic changes by famed French artist Marc Chagall, is among the most brilliant pieces of public art in Chicago. Sitting on the floor of the Bank One Plaza, Chagall's colorful work stretches some 14 feet high, 70 feet in length, and 10 feet wide.*

▶▶ **Chicago Skyline:** *This view from Lake Michigan displays the eastern edge of Chicago's Grant Park. Dominating the skyline is the Sears Tower by Skidmore Owings and Merrill, America's tallest building. This view allows the various height levels of Chicago buildings to be seen. Just beneath the Sears Tower is the Chicago Board of Trade, the city's tallest building in the 1930s. Architecture remains an important part of Chicago life.*

college education. He remains the most significant political personality in Chicago's history.

In the ensuing decades, Chicago politics have produced political leaders expressive of the imperatives of the times. Jane Byrne served as the city's first woman mayor in the late 1970s, and Harold Washington became the city's first African-American mayor in the 1980s. Richard M. Daley, the son of the previous Mayor Daley, was elected in the late 1980s and has gone on to set a record for longevity and urban success that rivals his father.

In the meantime, Chicago continues to thrive with unprecedented municipal achievements. Richard M. Daley's reputation as a "Green" mayor has ensured that Chicago botanicals outdo any other city in the nation. The construction of Millennium Park has produced the most splendid urban landscape in the country, all produced in a partnership with corporate philanthropy that has allowed an extravagant architectural wonder to unfold, led by Frank Gehry's Pritzker Pavillion and Anish Kapoor's "Cloud Gate."

Chicago continues to progress unheralded urban redesign. New neighborhoods ring the city center. Commercial properties are transformed into domestic residences of fresh designs. A population "boom" is reinventing the local landscape. Surrounded by an energetic program in the arts, restaurants of remarkable quality, and an urban confidence that is unmatched in the city's history, a steady flow of people are returning to city living by choice.

The tempo of Chicago life is sound and inviting. It is ironic that the two institutions that always play to sold-out crowds are the Chicago Cubs and the Lyric Opera. This displays one of the great insights into Chicago's Prairie personality and quirky character. It is the city in which the atom was first split, the world's first blood bank was opened, the Chicago Symphony Orchestra holds court, and its Art Institute has more French Impressionist paintings than any other museum outside Paris. But it is also the city that gave the world the Hostess Twinkie, deep-dish pizza, the Duncan Yo-Yo, and the zipper. Chicago might enjoy the panache of its sophisticated persona at times, but it just does so without taking itself too seriously.

The Loop

Chicago's central business district takes its name from the ring of elevated train tracks that have encircled "downtown" for more than a century. The city's commercial center, however, has expanded well beyond the confines of this nineteenth century rail footprint. The "EL" is among one of Chicago's most enduring landmarks. The tracks run up Lake Street on the north; Wabash Street on the east; Van Buren on the South and Wells Street on the west. Neo-classical City Hall, as well Helmut Jahn's startling State of Illinois Building, shares the neighborhood with robust banking and financial institutions, like the Chicago Board of Trade and other Future Exchanges. All make their home "in the Loop." Generally, Chicagoans define the Loop as the city's historic center for shopping, commerce, business, and cultural institutions south of the Chicago River. Silk stocking law firms, the federal courts, the theater district, along with many vintage hotels, the Art Institute, the main Chicago Public Library, the Lyric Opera, and Millennium Park all are within the shadow of the Loop.

This neighborhood is home to America's most dramatic skyline. Underground a network of subway lines carries passengers across the city. DePaul University, the School of the Art Institute, Columbia College, and Roosevelt University each hold an important academic presence here. So, too, do vintage department stores along State Street, like Marshall Field & Company, the flagship for high end outfitting since before the Fire of 1871. Field's distinctive clocks have been the meeting spot for Chicagoans for generations. Carson Pirie Scott is a prestigious department store that occupies a singular building designed by architect Louis Sullivan. The Sears Tower is the king of all buildings in the Loop, as well as the country. Designed by Skidmore Owings and Merrill, the firm can count many historic high-rise buildings among its modern works, none more shimmering that the polished steel and green glass Inland Steel Building on Monroe Street. The Federal Plaza, a series of remarkable black steel and glass buildings by Ludwig Mies van der Rohe—who invented the city's modern architectural persona—may just be the finest collection of his style in the world.

Public art is displayed in the Loop with drama and surprising sophistication. Pablo Picasso got the ball rolling when he made a gift of "A Woman," a towering rusty female face, to the people of Chicago almost 40 years ago because he delighted in the style of Mayor Richard J. Daley. It sits in the plaza of the Daley Center, home to the Circuit Court. Marc Chagall's "Four Seasons," Alexander Calder's "Flamingo," and Joan Miro's "Standing Woman," are just the tip of the

▶ **Jay Pritzker Pavilion, Millennium Park:** *Architect Frank Gehry's Jay Pritzker Pavilion is the anchor of Chicago's Millennium Park. The titanium super-structure sits beneath other architectural landmarks from other eras. On the left is the Prudential Building, the city's tallest skyscraper in 1959. On the western façade is Alfonso Ianelli's Rock of Gibraltar sculptural relief from the eighth to the eleventh floors. Just behind the building is its shimmering Prudential Tower II built in the 1990s. To the right is Chicago's second tallest structure, the AON Building. In the foreground sits the Great Lawn of Millennium Park and the skeletal tubes that provide crisp sound throughout musical performances.*

◀ **Millennium Park:**
Architect Frank Gehry's titanium footbridge snakes across Columbus Drive on the east end of Millennium Park, connecting it to the lakefront. Looking west, the skyline rises above the park along Michigan Avenue.

▶ **Harold Washington Library:** *The city's main public library runs along State Street and was named in honor of the city's first African-American mayor, during whose office the library was first proposed. Chicago architect Thomas Beeby, of Hammond, Beeby and Babka, created a postmodern monolith displaying a wide variety of Chicago styles. Rau Kaskey's 12-foot Barn Owls are perched on the building's four corners, while a 20-foot Horned Owl hovers above the entrance of the largest public library in the world.*

◀ **Cloud Gate, Millennium Park:**
Dominating the grandeur of Chicago's Millennium Park is "Cloud Gate," the stunning sculpture by Anglo-Indian artist Anish Kapoor. In the remarkable curving surface of the "bean," as locals refer to it, the panorama of the surrounding cityscape appears in unusual reflected imagery. Visitors can pass beneath its curved interior, while artists ring its exterior painting new and extraordinary perspectives of Chicago.

◀ ◀ **Chicago River:** *A westward view of the Chicago River from the Michigan Avenue Bridge, south bank on the left, north bank on the right. The land here gave birth to Chicago at this juncture where the prairie meets the lake. Mies van der Rohe's soaring glass and steel IBM tower dominates the north side. The Rococo temples atop the 35 West Wacker building, on the south bank, share the sky with other urban masterpieces. River traffic continues to shuttle both tourists and commuters.*

◀ **Sears Tower:** *At 110 stories, Skidmore Owings and Merrill's Sears Tower remains the king of the Chicago skyline and North America's tallest building. Its architectural wonder evolved out of the city's passion for commercial structures of both form and utility. The building has the world's highest occupied floors, and at four-and-a-half-million square feet, remains the world's largest skyscraper.*

▶ **State Street:** *Chicago Theater has dominated the flashy character of State Street since 1921. Its neon signage is a historic landmark today. After decades of use as a movie theater, it is once again an anchor of live theater productions.*

◄ **Grant Park:** *Named to honor the hero who saved the Union, commanding federal troops to victory in the Civil War, Illinois native Ulysses S. Grant, Grant Park has been called Chicago's "front yard." It forms part of the 27-mile long string of lakefront parks that run along the urban coastline. In the aftermath of the Great Fire in 1871, it was used as the dumping ground for the charred detritus of the disaster.*

▲ **The Art Institute of Chicago:** *The city's most famous lions, on guard at the Art Institute of Chicago, are the work of sculptor Edward Kemeys. Since 1894, they have added great majesty to the building that houses more than 300,000 works of art, including more French Impressionist paintings than any other city in the world outside of Paris. The original structure was built for the 1893 World's Fair and its classical style provides a taste of the way the fair looked.*

◀ **Daley Plaza:** *Officially "untitled," Chicago's first and most famous piece of modern outdoor public art was a gift to the city from its creator, Pablo Picasso. It stands in the plaza of the Daley Center housing the Cook County Circuit Court. Unveiled in 1967, the Cor-Ten steel figure* *stands 55 feet tall and weighs 162 tons. Many see a reflection of the artist's female heads that fill his work. Once highly controversial, it is now as much a part of Chicago's life as the Cubs.*

▲ **Dearborn Station:** *The Dearborn Street Station is the city's only surviving nineteenth-century railway station. Designed by architect Cyrus W. Elditz in 1883, as the Chicago and Western Indiana Railway Station, it reflects the grandeur and might of Chicago's railway* *past when the rail lines of the nation all passed through Chicago. Today, it has been renovated into a thriving commercial space of shops and restaurants. The former rail yards surrounding it are now a bustling urban residential neighborhood.*

▲ **Buckingham Fountain:** *An extravagant landmark of colored lights and sky shooting geysers, the Buckingham Fountain is right out of the Court of Louis XIV. The fountain was a gift from Chicago philanthropist Kate Buckingham to honor her brother Clarence. It is located in Grant Park near the lakefront and has been the city's premier showpiece since its 1927 unveiling.*

▲ **Civic Opera House:**
Designed by Alfred Shaw for Graham, Anderson, Probst & White, the architectural heirs of Daniel Burnham, the Civic Opera House was the brainchild of utility baron Samuel Insull. Built beside the south branch of the Chicago River, along Wacker Drive, it opened in 1929 and contained a 45-story office building, as well as an opera house and theater. Today the building is home to the city's famed Lyric Opera.

▶ **Buddy Guy's Legends:** *This legendary venue is one of the United States' best-loved live music venues. As well as serving great home-cooked food, its stage has been visited by a roll-call of the world's favorite musicians, from Mick Jagger, David Bowie, and Eric Clapton, to Muddy Waters, B.B. King, and Carlos Santana. Buddy himself is often to be found jamming with friends onstage.*

◀ **Union Station:** *The city's great riverfront Beaux Arts 1920s railway station houses both Amtrak and the vast network of commuter lines. Designed by architect Pierce Anderson of Graham, Anderson, Probst & White, the protégées of Daniel Burnham, Union Station is an urban landmark and a prime venue for social and charity events.*

▶ **Museum Campus:** *The city's lakefront museum campus, anchored by the Shedd Aquarium and the Adler Planetarium, sits near the Burnham Harbor site of the 1933 World's Fair—"The Century of Progress." Each opened at the start of the 1930s and reflects the philanthropy of Chicago fortunes. Both have also received substantial expansions that continue to make them highly popular Chicago destinations.*

▶ **Chicago Cultural Center:** *Originally built in 1897 as the city's main Public Library, the Chicago Cultural Center was designed in the Italian Renaissance style by Shepley, Rutan & Coolidge. Today it serves as a focal point for the city's vast network of cultural programs. A great Tiffany glass dome roofs one of the galleries. Once scheduled for destruction in the late 1960s, it was saved by the direct intervention of Eleanor Daley, wife of Mayor Richard J. Daley.*

◄ **Symphony Center:**
Orchestra Hall was designed by Chicago's premier architect Daniel Burnham and opened in 1904. Built on stately Michigan Avenue not far from the Art Institute, it is known today as Symphony Center and is the home of the world famous Chicago Symphony Orchestra, which holds a record number of prestigious Grammy Awards for their recordings.

▶ **Monadnock Building:**
Built between 1889 and 1893, the Monadnock Building is actually two connected, though distinctive, wings and from two eras of Chicago design. The older, northern end was designed by Daniel Burnham and John Wellborn Root and uses load-bearing walls that gave it a distinctive thick walled design. The south end was deigned by William Holabird and Martin Roche using steel frame construction.

▶▶ **The Rookery:** *The grand dame of Chicago urban design, the Rookery was originally designed by Daniel Burnham and John Wellborn Root in 1885 and was named for a bird roost that once occupied the site. Frank Lloyd Wright had an office here around the turn of the century and carried out a renovation of the lobby area in 1905 that gave the atrium a distinctive Prairie character.*

The Rookery: The grand dame of Chicago urban design, the Rookery was originally designed by Daniel Burnham and John Wellborn Root in 1885 and was named for a bird roost that once occupied the site. Frank Lloyd Wright had an office here around the turn of the century and carried out a renovation of the lobby area in 1905 that gave the atrium a distinctive Prairie character.

▲ **Federal Buildings:**
Alexander Calder's bold
orangey-pink 53-foot
"Flamingo" has stood in the
modernist plaza of Mies van
der Rohe's Federal Buildings
since 1974. It is the perfect

compliment to their black Cor-
Ten designs. Calder came to
town for the unveiling,
simultaneous with that of his
mobile in the lobby of the
Sears Tower.

▶ **Reliance Building:**
The Burnham Hotel's interior
foyer and elevator bank along
State Street. Originally built in
1895 as the Reliance Building,
today it has been refashioned
into a boutique hotel bearing

Burnham's name. This is the
world's very first glass-and-
steel-frame commercial high-
rise. From this one all others
descend.

▶ **The Thompson Center:** *Jean Dubuffet's 29-foot-tall fiberglass sculpture intrigues passers-by in the plaza outside The Thompson Center. This politically designed building is the State of Illinois's official headquarters in Chicago. Designed by architect Helmut Jahn in 1985, it is a controversial postmodernist glass dome in which the inner-workings of government are meant to be seen.*

◀ **Fine Arts Building:** *Designed by Solon S. Berman in 1885 as the Studebaker Building, the building on South Michigan Avenue was originally a showroom for automobiles. It later became known as the Fine Arts Building and its 11 stories have been the heart of Chicago's art community for musicians, artists, bookmakers, and singers throughout its 65-plus studios. Among its tenants have been sculptor Laredo Taft; painter Hazel, Lady Lavery; cartoonist John T. McCutcheon; and popular bookstores.*

▶ **Printer's Row:** *Once home to the city's vast commercial printing economy, now this neighborhood in the South Loop has morphed residential, a good example of the urban transformation Chicago has produced. Lofts abound in this area conveniently adjacent to the nearby Loop.*

▶ **LaSalle Street:**

Named for the seventeenth-century French explorer the Chevalier Robert Sur LaSalle, LaSalle Street is the city's financial canyon, anchored on the south end by the famed Chicago Board of Trade, the soaring 1930 Art Deco granite masterpiece of Holabird and Root. The grains and agricultural commodities of the heartland are traded on its "floors."

◄ **Auditorium Building:** *This was the tallest building in the world when it opened in 1886, as well as the earliest mixed-use building. Louis Sullivan and Dankmar Adler opened a new era of Chicago design here with the opera house, hotel, and commercial high-rise. The tower was home to their firm through which they employed a youthful Frank Lloyd Wright.*

► **Berghoff Café:** *The Berghoff on Adams Street is Chicago's oldest surviving German restaurant. The eatery began at the World's Columbian Exposition of 1893. Famous for brewing their own beer and baking their own rye bread, The Berghoff is a landmark feature in Chicago, housed in a row of Italianate buildings built immediately following the Great Fire of 1871.*

► **Marquette Building:** *This vintage Chicago commercial high-rise was built in 1895. No building displays the traditional "Chicago window" with more panache. Taking its name from the French Jesuit explorer who wintered in the area in 1673, the interior of the Marquette Building showcases such early Chicago history through a series of panels executed in gleaming bronze. Prairie proportion is beautifully utilized here.*

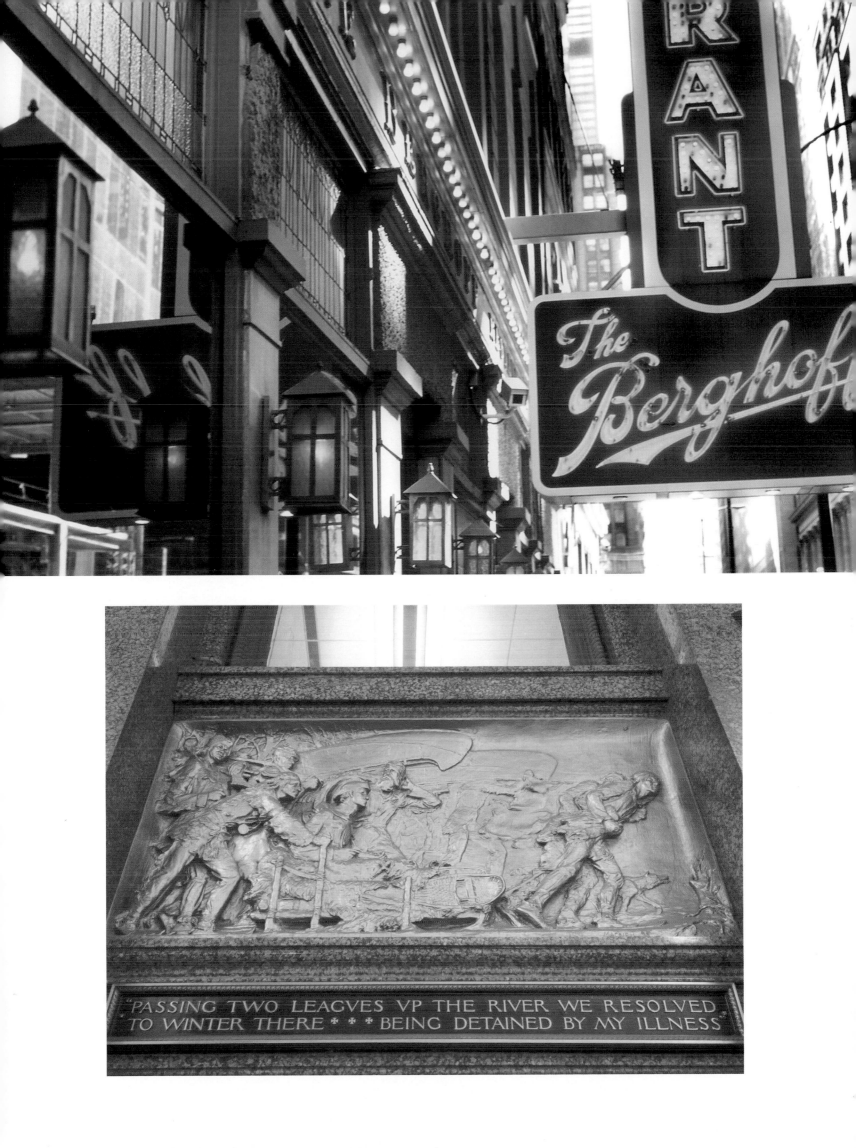

**◄▲ Prudential
Building:** *The first
Prudential Building, at 41
stories, was Chicago's tallest
skyscraper when it was
opened in 1955. Viewed from
beyond the Buckingham
Fountain (left) it is located at
One Prudential Plaza and was
designed by Naess and
Murphy. Towering over it*
*(above) is its neighbor at Two
Prudential Plaza— sometimes
known as "2 Pru." Designed
by Loehl, Schlossman and
Hackl. the second Prudential
building is a 64-story structure
completed in 1990. Together
they occupy more than three
acres along the Randolph
Street border of Millennium
Park.*

North of the River

The Chicago River cuts into the landscape with power and precision. Since New Year's Day 1900, it has flowed from Lake Michigan, forking into a "Y," with a south and north branch. The reversal of the river's flow is among the greatest feats of engineering in American history. The river's south passage once connected the city to the Illinois & Michigan canal, serving as an important commercial shipping route. The north branch bends at the Merchandise Mart, the largest commercial building in the world, and takes a northwest route through the city. Each branch is a busy thoroughfare for boaters to and from the lake.

Commercial life was minimal on the north side of the river until two important buildings transformed the character of this part of town. The Wrigley Building and the Tribune Tower altered the tone of the neighborhood when their famous designs were conceived and built on Michigan Avenue in the 1920s. Wrigley's White rococo style and the Tribune's gothic medievalism stand as the gateways to a new era of Chicago commerce on the river's other shore. Over the next half century business life expanded. Today, this area is Chicago's most dynamic and high- end shopping in town.

Two historic landmarks further up shape the character of Michigan Avenue—the wedding cake-like Illinois limestone Water Tower that remains the only structure to survive the Great Fire of 1871. Nearby, the John Hancock Center cuts into the sky, the home of sophisticated commercial and residential properties.

Oak Street Beach is Chicago's own version of Copacabana or Ipanema. This mini-Riviera faces the city's most exclusive luxury buildings—East Lake Shore Drive. Oak Street itself is home to fancy boutiques and designer showcase shopping. Just north, along North Lake Shore Drive, is "the Gold Coast:" a small enclave of elegance along Astor Street, State Parkway, and Dearborn Street. Historic homes are plentiful and nearby Lincoln Park provides a scenic panorama. Residents include the Roman Catholic Cardinal, as well as socialites, debutantes, industrial barons, and Oprah Winfrey.

The Four Seasons, the Drake, and the Peninsula are the neighborhood's luxury hotels, alongside Saks Fifth Avenue, Ralph Lauren, Gucci, and Tiffany. Famous restaurants abound, including RL, Gibsons, Hugo's Frog Bar and the wall-to-wall streetscape of saloons along Division Street. Butch McGuire's is perhaps the area's most famous watering hole. Close by is Loyola University's urban campus, as well as the Museum of Contemporary Art and the vast expanse of Northwestern University's medical campus and law school.

▶ **Chicago Water Tower and John Hancock Center:** *Chicago's most two famous towers are neighbors on Michigan Avenue—W. W. Boyington's castellated Water Tower of 1869, and Skidmore Owing and Merrill's soaring Cor-Ten steel-framed John Hancock Center of 1969. The Water Tower is actually a 138-foot standpipe designed to enhance the water intake from Lake Michigan, but its ability to survive the Great Fire gave it a historical significance that now transcends its original purpose. The Hancock Center is a Chicago landmark of slender urban grace.*

◀ **Chicago Tribune Tower:** *Situated along Michigan Avenue on the north bank of the Chicago River, the Chicago Tribune Tower rises 438 feet, like a medieval cathedral above the prairie. The work of architects Raymond Hood and John Howells in 1922, the design beat 260 others in an international competition for the newspaper's new headquarters.*

▶ **Wrigley Building:** *This impressive building by Graham, Anderson, Probst & White, built in 1921, began the commercial revitalization of the land north of the Chicago River along Michigan Avenue. The headquarters of the chewing gum empire is actually two buildings; a 32-story south building and tower, as well as a 21-story north building. Built in the Spanish Rococo style, the Wrigley Building's Moorish design is reminiscent of the Giralda Tower of the fifteenth-century tower of the Cathedral of Seville.*

◀ **Water Tower Place:**
*This 65-story commercial and
residential complex along
North Michigan Avenue
includes a seven-story mall of
high-end shopping, the Ritz-
Carlton Hotel, and a variety of
restaurants. Marshall Field &
Company and Lord and Taylor
anchor its commercial appeal.*

▶ **Drake Hotel:** *A
Chicago legend designed by
architects Benjamin Marshall
and Charles Fox in 1919. In a
vintage neighborhood of elite
addresses, this landmark
overlooks the Chicago Riviera,
Oak Street Beach. The hotel
has welcomed kings, queens
and presidents, as well as
Gold Coast debutantes and
trust-fund preppies.*

▶ **North Michigan
Avenue:** *On the left of this
view looking north from the
Michigan Avenue Bridge is
the Wrigley Building and on
the right is the Tribune Tower.
They were the gateway to the
street's commercial
development and the
catalysts for fine architectural
design north of the river.*

▶ ▶ **Navy Pier:** *Built as
a military facility in the era of
World War I, Navy Pier served
as home to the University of
Illinois after World War II.
Despite periods of dereliction,
it was reborn in the 1990s
and today is a major
attraction for theater,
amusements, lake sailings,
and gala soirées.*

PAVILION

PAVILION

Navy Pier IMAX Theater
Chicago Children's Museum
Crystal Garden
Restaurants
Shops
Food Court

CHICAGO
CHILDREN'S
MUSEUM

◄ Newberry Library:
This public non-circulating library for scholars in the humanities and family genealogy was designed by Henry Ives Cobb in the Romanesque revivalist style and opened to the public in 1892 on Walton Street between Dearborn and Clark streets. Named for Chicago real estate tycoon Walter Loomis Newberry, whose fortune financed the library, it was inspired by the twelfth-century French church of Saint Giles-du-Gard.

► John Hancock Building: *This 100-story building at 870 North Michigan Avenue has been a signature piece of Chicago real estate since the mid-1960s. Bruce Graham of Skidmore, Owings and Merrill designed it, with the genius of engineer Fazlur Kahn to guide him. The building—one of the tallest in the world at 1,127 feet—combines commercial space on the lower 50 floors and residential on the upper 50.*

► Museum of Contemporary Art:
Designed by architect Josef Paul Kleihues, the museum opened in its new home in Streeterville in 1996. With some 115,000 square feet of interior space, it houses a remarkable permanent collection, as well as an outdoor sculpture garden.

◀ **Marina City:** *Designed by architect Bertrand Goldberg in 1964, Marina City introduced a radical new concept in urban living. Rising on the north bank of the Chicago River, it marked the beginning of residential living in the commercial city center. Goldberg's concrete twin towers resemble ears of corn by their scalloped design and contained all essential urban necessities from groceries and dry cleaning to restaurants and a bowling alley.*

▶ **House of Blues:** *Located in what was originally the commercial office building built alongside Marina City, House of Blues is both a hotel and a performance venue located along State Street north of the river. Top name musicians and bands fill the stage regularly.*

◀ **Billy Goat Tavern:** *This renowned watering hole is a staple of "underground" North Michigan Avenue life, the streetscape that runs beneath that thoroughfare. Popularized by generations of reporters and staffers from the Chicago Tribune, founder Sam Sianis, an immigrant from Greece, offered a staple, but limited, menu; "Cheeeeezeburgers, cheeeeeezeburgers." Sianis is also credited as the man who used his Billy Goat to lay a curse on the Chicago Cubs.*

Dear Ruby,

This was a scary day for Flat Stanley.
He tried to help me in the garden, but a big
gust of wind came along and blew him right out into
the street. Luckily no car came along, and I
was able ~~to run over and bring him~~ catch him.

He wasn't hurt, He just got a little dirty, but
he's a boy so I don't think he minds that. We
learned that there are lots of things a flat
fellow can do, but ~~sitting~~ helping in a the garden on a windy
day isn't one of them.

2481 ANDERSON LAKE RD
CHIMACUM, WA
98325
EASTER SUNDAY
APRIL 12, 2009

DEAR RUBY,

THANK YOU SO MUCH FOR SENDING FLAT
STANLEY TO VISIT ME. HE CAME WITH ME TO EASTER
DINNER WHERE WE HAD LAMB, HAM, MASHED POTATOES,
GREEN BEANS AND SALAD. ~~AND~~ AND, OF COURSE, DESSERT,
FLAT STANLEY LIKE ~~DESSERT~~ DESSERT BEST JUST LIKE GRANDMA
PAT.

HE MET MY FRIENDS JOANNA AND WIL AND THEIR
DOG BOJO. BOJO IS A BLACK STANDARD POODLE WHO
LOVES EVERYBODY AND HE LOVED FLAT STANLEY SO
MUCH HE TRIED TO LICK HIM. DON'T WORRY! I'M PRETTY
QUICK FOR A GRANDMA AND I SAVED ~~FLAT~~ STANLEY
SO HE CAN GO ON MORE ADVENTURES WITH ME.

I'LL WRITE AGAIN NEXT WEEK TO LET YOU KNOW
WHAT NEW ADVENTURES STANLEY AND I ARE HAVING.

LOVE YOU,
GP

ON WEDNESDAYS I WORK AT A STORE CALLED H F H Furniture
and more store. People give us ^nice things they no ~~longer~~ need and we sell
them to help make money so our volunteers can partner with people who
need houses. Each person must ~~work~~ work for 400 hours ^on ~~of our~~ our
projects before they can qualify for a house. We hope to build 4 ^houses ~~this~~
~~summer~~.

Flat Stanley sat (well, leaned) right by the cash register
and greeted people. Here are some of the people who said "hello"
to him.

He helped me not ~~to~~ make any mistakes at the cash register.
I'm sure glad ~~you sent him home~~ you sent him to ~~for~~ me.

Flat Stanley ~~and I have been trying to~~

Flat Stanley can hardly wait (for me) to send you this letter. He went to the Seattle Art Museum with your cousin Jenna and me last Saturday. ~~Jenna~~ He didn't even need a ticket.

Jenna's favorite exhibit was ____ but Flat Stanley was most impressed by the ____ sculpture ~~Flat Stanley and I have been trying to find the best place for him to sit in the truck as we start our trip. We are going to do some camping up near the Canadian border but~~ made up of ~~the~~ metal dog tags. The dog tags are as (individual) flat as Stanley but when the artist put them ~~all~~ together he made this huge ____.

Stanley was wondering what we could make ~~out of~~ (if we had) ~~all~~ flat people like him. We'll have to think about that.

Have you ever heard of a special seat belt for someone like Flat Stanley? Well, pretty soon you will get to see one. We needed a seat belt so Stanley could see out the window as we drive along on our camping trip. He wants you to know he has been very brave riding up on the dashboard because the logging trucks are really big and when one goes past us Stanley gets blown this way and that. He doesn't complain, but I think he is glad when we stop for the night and he can come into the camper.

Tomorrow we are going to walk across the Deception Pass Bridge. It is very high and we'll be able to look straight down at the rushing water below. I wonder how Stanley will like this adventure.

◀ **Merchandise Mart:**
*Built in 1930 by Graham,
Anderson, Probst and White,
the Merchandise Mart is in the
heart of vintage Chicago: Wolf
Point. Spanning two city blocks,
it was the concept of Marshall
Field IV; it was created as a
wholesale commercial center
for the nation. Spanning over
4,100,000 square feet, it was
the world's largest building until
the construction of the
Pentagon.*

▼ **Holy Name
Cathedral:** *This is the
mother church of the Roman
Catholic Archdiocese of
Chicago. Located on North
State Street, the Holy Name
Cathedral was among one of
the earliest structures to be
rebuilt following the Great
Fire of 1871. Designed by
Patrick Charles Keeley, it is
constructed of yellow Illinois
limestone, much like the
historic Water Tower nearby*

▲ **900 North Michigan Avenue:** *The building designed by Kohl, Pedersen, Fox in the mid-1980s at this address is more commonly referred to as "Bloomingdale's," as they are the shopping center's anchor tenant. The structure is actually a high mixed-use building housing other retail, commercial, residential, and hotel space, with the Four Seasons providing a five-star service.*

▶ **"The Magnificent Mile":** *The eight-block expanse of Michigan Avenue from the Chicago River north to Oak Street is known as "the Magnificent Mile." Fashionable designers and high-end national chains from Saks Fifth Avenue, Tiffany, and Chanel, to Ferragamo and Gucci, make this the city's premier center for chic shopping.*

◀ **Rush Street:** *This area was once the nightclub heart of Chicago, the streets thick with saloons and smoky rooms made popular by the first names in American entertainment. Today, this Gold Coast neighborhood is more richly filled with high-end eateries, like Gibson's, the first name in Chicago steaks, and Hugo's Frog Bar next door.*

▶ **"The Magnificent Mile":** *This is the view of Michigan Avenue looking south from Chicago Avenue to the full panorama of the "Mag Mile," displaying the blend of the old vintage neighborhood—the Allerton Hotel, the Tribune Tower, the Women's Athletic Club, and the Wrigley Building—with newer additions like Chicago Place, Crate and Barrel, Neiman Marcus, and stately Ralph Lauren's Polo Store. The mixture offers Chicagoans some of the best commercial streetscape in the nation.*

The West Loop

The area known as the West Loop is a part of Chicago that has been transformed by the explosion of urban re-gentrification that has taken hold over the past 20 years. As the commercial muscle of the business district pushed west, its economic engine carried this historic part of old Chicago with it. This portion of the city was not engulfed in the Great Fire of 1871 and has been the immigration gateway for successive layers of ethnic groups; Chicago's oldest continuous-use public building, Old St. Patrick's Church, at Adams and Des Plaines, is the traditional homeland of the early Irish.

Urban transition took the neighborhood from residential to commercial in the early twentieth century. And at the end of the century, it returned to residential living as lofts and commercial structures were refashioned for a new generation of urban pioneers. Nearby "Little Italy" is more famous today for its restaurants than for its tough-guy personalities. The neighborhood once held a large enclave of Greek immigrants and their descendants, until the construction of the University of Illinois' campus forced most to relocate further northwest. The heart of historic Greek town remains situated along Halsted Street with an abundance of good restaurants. It was here, back in the 1960s, that two local Greek entrepreneurs created Gyros, the ground beef and lamb concoction that is now a familiar staple worldwide.

The south end of the West Loop area was the port of entry at the turn of the last century for Jewish immigrants from Europe, who subsequently established a wholesale commercial market off 12th Street, known as Maxwell Street, that only recently disappeared. Also near 12th Street (Roosevelt Road) is historic Holy Family Church and St. Ignatius College Prep founded by the Jesuits in pre-Fire Chicago. Among their parishioners was Mrs. Catherine O'Leary, falsely accused of responsibility for the Great Fire. Ironically, the Chicago Fire Academy now stands on the site of what was once her meager homestead.

Visitors to the West Loop are often overwhelmed by the wafting aroma of chocolate in the air—a residual of the nearby Blommer Chocolate factory on Des Plaines Avenue.

Among the anchors of the West Loop are the United Center, home of the Chicago Bulls basketball team, and HARPO Productions, home of the Oprah Winfrey Television show. The neighborhood is also thick with tony bistros and a growing number of art galleries housed in the generous loft buildings that abound in the area. The Art Institute of Chicago is also a neighbor with its Jackson Boulevard campus location.

▶ **Greektown:** *The peristyle of Ionic columns along Halsted Street—the main thoroughfare in what was once the heart of Greek life in Chicago—displays a classical element of Greektown's historic heritage. Lining both sides of the street for blocks, restaurants continue the traditions of Greek cuisine in an area that is now more popular than ever.*

◄ **Old St. Patrick's Church:** *The oldest continuous-use public building in Chicago, Old St. Patrick's Church is a landmark of the heart for Chicago's Irish, for whom this was the gateway to America in the years of the dreaded Irish Famine. Designed by Augustus Bauer and Asher Carter, the church opened its doors in 1856, ten years after the founding of the parish. Re-gentrification in the 1980s has restored the parish to its former glory and the church to its architectural highpoint as the largest use of Celtic design in the world.*

▲ **The Chicago Fire Academy:** *Located at Jefferson and DeKoven Streets, the Chicago Fire Academy just might be the city's most historically ironic structure. It sits on the site of what was once the farm of Mrs. Catherine O'Leary—* ground zero for the conflagration. Though now absolved of any responsibility for the fire, Mrs. O'Leary endured a "bum-rap" for more than a century. Egon Weiner's bronze sculpture, "Pillar of Fire," marks the site of the blaze's start.

▼ **Blommer Chocolate Company:** *Located at Des Plaines and Milwaukee Avenues, Blommer Chocolate Factory has been producing chocolate since 1939, delighting Chicagoans with the wafting aroma of pungent chocolate.*

◄ **Hull House:** *This house is a shrine to the enterprise and heart of two unique women—Jane Addams and Ellen Gates. Acquiring the property from real estate mogul Charles J. Hull in the 1880s, Addams and Star endeavored to provide much needed educational programs and social service assistance for the many immigrants staying at the house. Today, it is a tribute to their efforts and the Nobel Peace Prize awarded to Addams.*

▲ **Taylor Street:** *Found in the very heart of Chicago's vintage Italian community, which once brimmed with immigrants. Though Mother Cabrini's hospital is now a condominium and the neighborhood has been re-gentrified, old-fashioned neighborhood values still are preserved, great Italian eateries abound, and Mario still serves homemade Italian lemonade.*

◀ **Harpo Studios:** *These famous studios have brought this neighborhood untold celebrity thanks to Oprah Winfrey's enterprise. Washington Boulevard is regularly thick with lines of Oprah fans lined up for her shows. Her studio, however, retains a curious Chicago pedigree. Following the 1915 sinking of the Eastland, in the Chicago River, with a loss of more than 800 lives, this former armory was used as a morgue for victims. Studio employees claim that the ghosts of the passengers still haunt the studios and recount strange occurrences taking place there at night.*

▶ **Batcolumn:** *Claes Oldenburg's "Batcolumn," located in the plaza of the Harold Washington Social Security Administration Building at 600 West Washington, is a five-story, 100-foot, 20-ton salute to the American baseball bat. Could Chicago have a more appropriate piece of modern public sculpture?*

◀ **Manny's Deli:** *Manny's Coffee Shop at Roosevelt Road and Jefferson Street is in truth Chicago's most remarkable old fashioned kosher deli, a remnant of the nearby Maxwell Street wholesale garment district. Mile-high corn beef sandwiches are juicy, and the potato latkes have to be eaten to be believed.*

◄ **Garfield Park Conservatory:** *First opened in 1874, just three years after the Great Fire, the Garfield Park Conservatory is at 100 N. Central Park Avenue. The largest glass atrium in the world, the conservatory was the work of noted American designer Jens Jensen and is a timeless home for the rare botanicals, plants, and palms that flourish there.*

▲ **United Center:** *Known to many as "the house that Jordan built," which refers to the extraordinary Chicago Bull Michael Jordan, whose career on the basketball court transformed the game and the city. The arena sits across the street from what was the Chicago Stadium, longtime home of both the Bulls and the Chicago Blackhawks Hockey Team. Many exciting national presidential conventions were held at the old stadium, including Roosevelt's unprecedented third and fourth nominations.*

Near Northwest Side

The neighborhoods that make up this edgy, hip part of Chicago were once the homelands of great numbers of central and eastern Europeans. At one point the area actually supported the largest concentration of Polish nationals outside of Warsaw. Historically, Milwaukee Avenue, a great commercial street that runs diagonally through the city and out beyond its limits, has been the anchor of Polish heritage within Chicago for more than a century. Not far away, another of the city's diagonal thoroughfares, Lincoln Avenue, provided a similar focal point for the large German community in the city. Today the steeples of the great churches built by the Polish and German communities still tower above the trees. However, assimilation and time have transformed the original ethnic character of most. Many of the neighborhoods have undergone a dramatic urban transition. Given their close proximity to the center of the city, the value of property has increased; young urban professionals have reconfigured the local landscape.

In many antique parts of Chicago old neighborhoods are becoming new again. This is especially true in communities like Wicker Park and Bucktown, Ukrainian Village and East Village, Humboldt Park, and Logan Square. The convergence of cultures is more dramatic here than ever before. An expansive array of new restaurants fit the sophistication of new residents who have the income and the tastes for a more upmarket style. But the onion domes and golden domes of Byzantine cathedrals continue to mark the landscape.

The Near Northwest Side still retains some of the character of its former residents such as writers Nelson Algren and Saul Bellow who celebrated a more unforgiving Chicago in their work. Some of the old Chicago can still be found in the Polish delicatessens and taverns that have remained. Corner taverns have an authentic feel to them, even if they are filled with "hipsters." Resale stores along Milwaukee Avenue provide indispensable vintage clothing for the more "funky" percentage of the local residents.

Artists, writers, poets, small theater companies, and musicians are an important component of the local population. The architecture of the colorful past is treasured. Small streetscapes here and there hold secret troves of hidden gems of late nineteenth century design. Lush trees and gardens cover the landscape, including the stunning contours of Humboldt Park which were laid out by Jens Jensen, a brilliant naturalist and the architectural genius behind many of Chicago's lush public gardens.

▶ **Division Street Russian and Turkish Baths:** *The baths at 1916 West Division were once one part of a large network of public baths: a staple among the immigrant community often without the facilities for hot baths at home. First opened in 1907, this bathhouse is enjoying new popularity among the young urban professionals who now live nearby. It is also a favorite of the Reverend Jesse Jackson.*

 **Wicker Park:** *The six corners formed by the intersection of Milwaukee, North, and Damen Avenues within the Wicker Park neighborhood abound with quality restaurants, bars, and shops that formed part of the re-gentrification of an old Chicago community. Fine architecture compliments the streetscape that is home to hipsters and yuppies, as well as the remnant of multi-ethnic old-timers.*

▶ **The Paderewski House:** *This building at 2138 West Pierce sits on a stately street in Wicker Park and draws its name from a visit by the famed pianist, Ignace Jan Paderewski, who served as Poland's Prime Minister after World War I. He played the piano on the porch of this mansion during an official visit.*

◀ **Earwax Café:** *This popular vegetarian eatery, on Milwaukee Avenue in Wicker Park, reflects both the values and whimsy of the bustling polyglot neighborhood.*

▶ **Polish Museum of America:** *Based at Milwaukee Avenue and Augusta Boulevard, the Polish Museum of America manifests the neighborhood's vintage Chicago-Polish pedigree. Housed within the headquarters of the Polish Roman Catholic Union, a fraternal organization that influenced the Polish immigrant community, it is once again busy with an unprecedented influx of twenty-first-century Poles making Chicago their home.*

◀ **Margie's Candies:** *This should be an anthropologist's paradise, for truly time has stood still here. Margie's Candies, at Milwaukee and Western Avenues, has been a Chicago institution for more than 80 years. It is said to have been Al Capone's favorite ice cream establishment. Every sugary delight offered, from the ice cream to the hot fudge and the hand-dipped candies, is homemade. Ice cream creations are all served in giant white conch shell dishes, with each booth generating its own unique Chicago-style of eccentricity.*

▲ **Wicker Park neighborhood mural:** *This mural is on an external wall of Silver Cloud, a cozy eatery at Damen Avenue and Wabansia Street, a neighborhood staple in Wicker Park. The design by Chicago-based ART CHAOS reflects the sophisticated tastes of the neighborhood residents. Outdoor eating is an urban way of life here in clement weather.*

◄ **The Matchbox:** *At the corner of Milwaukee, Ogden, and Chicago Avenues, the Matchbox is the city's narrowest saloon. In these tight but friendly quarters locals display a bonhomie of unusual intimacy within a true Chicago classic.*

▲ **The Stables at Humboldt Park:** *Located within Humboldt Park, at 1400 North Sacramento Boulevard, The Stables reflect the historic grandeur envisioned by famed urban garden architect Jens Jensen, the creator of some of the city's most splendid parklands.*

It was designed in the Queen Anne-style of sturdy German aristocratic country motif by the firm of Fromann and Jebsen in 1896. The stables, together with other park buildings, are among the city's landmarks, displaying lasting utility and beauty.

The North Side

The North Side is the heartland of Chicago allegiance and citizenship. This is "Cub's territory." Chicagoans know they are on the North Side when they see that all the city street signs have names, rather than numbers. Belmont Avenue, for example, crosses Ashland Avenue. On the South Side, streets like Ashland are intersected by 22nd Street, or 35th Street, or 95th Street. That's just how it is in the network of neighborhoods here, like Lincoln Park, Wrigleyville, DePaul, Lakeview, Uptown, Roscoe Village, Andersonville, Lincoln Square, and Rogers Park.

Lincoln Park takes its name from the lakefront acreage that is the city's tribute to the slain 16th President of the United States. Lincoln's body stopped in Chicago on its way to burial in the state capital at Springfield in 1865. City leaders decided to create the park as a tribute to him. Before it became a park, the land held the city's cemetery. Thousands of bodies had to be moved to create the park—the soggy ground did not make much of a cemetery then. As the project was underway, the Great Fire of 1871 began. Many local residents sought refuge from the flames by jumping into the empty graves. Today, the park contains the oldest free zoo in America, as well as a nature museum, jogging paths, and a great glass botanical conservatory.

Wrigley Field is ground zero for Chicago sports fans in a neighborhood that embodies the very essence of Chicago baseball. The many apartment buildings here are filled with young urban professionals drawn by the easy commute downtown on the "EL" and the extraordinary number of saloons that line the streets. The nearby DePaul University is one of the nation's fastest growing academic institutions. Once a commuter school, it is now a leader in first choice applications.

Further north, neighborhoods are undergoing unprecedented revival; it is hip to live in the city. Uptown boasts a large Vietnamese population: at the Argyle Avenue "EL" stop a pagoda-roofed station welcomes riders. Andersonville, north of Foster Avenue, was settled by Swedish immigrants and still reflects the characteristic style of the Scandinavian culture. Big wooden-framed Victorian and Edwardian houses are highly sought after.

"Boys Town" is home to the city's large gay community around Halsted and Belmont and hosts the Pride Parade every June. Just to the north, in Rogers Park, Loyola University's campus sprawls along the lakefront, and further west along Devon Avenue a significant South Asian Indian population has transformed the community with exotic stores and restaurants.

Many communities on the North Side were once independent towns in the nineteenth century and annexed themselves to Chicago before the turn of the century.

▶ **Southport Lanes & Billiards:** *Continuing to emit the same old-fashioned charm it did when the neighborhood was home to the city's hardworking German residents, Southport Lanes & Billiards has been a neighborhood institution since 1922. More of a bar with a bowling alley attached, today, it is an anchor of the revival that re-gentrification has brought about. The bowling here is vintage: strictly manual lanes.*

◄ **Superdawg Drive-In:** *For more than 50 years Superdawg Drive-In, on North Milwaukee Avenue, has served some of Chicago's finest "Chicago-Dogs," as the city's unique version of the American hot-dog is known. Car-hops still serve customers in their cars and orders are placed over two-way speakers. It is generational tradition for many families who delight in eating off a tray hooked to their car windows. This is true vintage Chicago.*

◀ **Graceland Cemetery:** *The final resting place of some of Chicago's most notable citizens, Graceland Cemetery at 4001 North Clark Street residents include early pioneers, like John Kinzie, as well as its* *commercial titans, like Marshall Field, Potter Palmer, and George Pullman. Perhaps its most famous tomb is the Prairie-style Getty Mausoleum (1890) by Louis Sullivan located not far from where the architect himself is buried.*

▲ **Music Box Theater:** *This classic 1920s Chicago neighborhood "movie palace" on North Southport Avenue is now a rare item since the introduction of the "multiplex." But this is a sacred shrine for those who revere cinema.* *Connoisseurs treasure the edgy independent films shown there, as well as revivals of classic films.*

▲ **Green Mill Tavern:** As Chicago's oldest continuously operating nightclub (on North Broadway Avenue), the Green Mill Tavern is a vintage slice of Chicago culture—both literary and criminal. Well-known today as the hip home of "Poetry Slams," an open microphone cabaret event of fast-paced guerilla poetry performance, during the 1920s this establishment had ties to Al Capone and his underworld empire of illegal bootlegging.

▶ **Café Brauer:** This picturesque café is situated in the heart of Lincoln Park, on Stockton Drive, overlooking the zoo and the lagoon. The Prairie School-designed landmark building offers a 4,000-square-foot hall for events and parties is in a setting of unequaled Chicago majesty.

◄◄ **Lincoln Park Zoo:**

Nestled in the heart of Lincoln Park is America's last free zoo. Encompassing a vast 35 acres, Lincoln Park Zoo has over 4 million visitors a year who come to this urban treasure to view more than 1900 permanent animal residents. "Bushman," America's most famous gorilla, was the zoo's most well known inhabitant for many years.

◄ **Uptown Theater:**

This is a true Chicago landmark. Located on North Broadway, this Spanish Revivalist-designed theater was the center of the great empire of motion picture palaces operated by the Balaban and Katz chain in the 1920s. At one time it was the second largest theater in America with 4500 seats: only Radio City Music Hall was larger.

▶ **North Avenue Beach Chess Pavilion:**

With its unusual outdoor venue, the North Avenue Beach Chess Pavilion is a lakefront feature that attracts scores of chess fans. Designed in 1957 using flat surfaces of poured concrete in the modernist style, by architect Morris Webster, the pavilion also includes two five-foot granite statues, a chess king and queen, by Boris Gilbertson.

◀ Chicago Historical Society: *Located on North Clark Street, the Chicago Historical Society holds a rich depository of the city's treasures—from Abraham Lincoln's death bed and John Dillinger's wooden gun to an evening gown worn by Mrs. Potter Palmer. It also houses a remarkable library of Chicago history and events centering on life in the city which makes the society's collection an important tool for understanding the city's urban character.*

▶ India Town: *Devon Avenue—"Little India"—in the East Rogers Park neighborhood has become an exotic and enticing home for thousands of east Indians. With them has come a variety of restaurants and food stores, as well as spice merchants who are scattered throughout the community just west of Loyola University's lakeshore campus.*

◀ Peggy Notebaert Nature Museum: *Positioned near the shores of Lake Michigan in Lincoln Park, the Peggy Notebaert Nature Museum, at Fullerton Avenue and Cannon Drive, is Chicago's newest and most unusual museum. The year-round butterfly haven is one of its biggest attractions.*

▲ **Swedish American Museum:** *This museum, on North Clark Street, is a treasure trove of Swedish cultural life in Chicago. Since 1976 it has endeavored to keep alive the traditions and* contributions of Swedes in the U.S. Swedish immigrants first arrived in Chicago in 1846 and the community experienced unprecedented growth due to further immigration in the 1880s.

▶ **Andersonville:** *The area surrounding Foster Avenue and Clark Street has been a home to Swedish Chicagoans for many generations. The neat streets of clapboard homes and* elegant gardens have always been prized real estate. This leafy community brims with good restaurants, pubs, boutique shops, and old Swedish markets.

▶ **Chris's Billiards:** *This is the "last of its kind" in Chicago—a true pool hall. Chris's Billiards, at 4637 North Milwaukee Avenue, has been offering its patrons quality leisure time for more than 35 years. Spread out through three rooms are 48 tables of real quality— "Brunswick Gold Crown." Chicagoans can step back into another era of urban life and shoot pool with "Belgium Championship Balls," every day of the year from 9 am to 2 am.*

◀ **Wrigley Field:** *"The Friendly Confines," or Wrigley Field, is home to the Chicago Cubs. One of the last great vintage stadiums in Major League Baseball, Wrigley Field is sacred soil; few of the city's landmarks hold the hearts of so many Chicagoans. Built in 1914, the team and the stadium were purchased by Chicago chewing gum-magnate William Wrigley, Jr., in 1920. Its ivy covered walls, for which it is famous, were added in 1937.*

◄ **Old Town School of Folk Music:** *Now located outside of the Old Town neighborhood, along Lincoln Avenue near Lincoln Square, this has been a Chicago institution for more than half a century, expanding the loyalties of folk music and performance enthusiasts through a commitment to music education and to the values of folk traditions.*

▶ **Vic Theatre:** *Built in 1912 as a vaudeville house, the Vic Theater on North Sheffield is now the home of live music with quality bands performing here. But when no live production is underway, it is transformed into "Brew&View," a unique movie theater with three bars in which patrons sing along or dance along to the dialogue.*

▶ **Biograph Theater:** *For many years the Biograph Theater, on 2433 North Lincoln Avenue, was an ordinary movie theater, until "Public Enemy Number One", John Dillinger, was gunned down in the adjacent alley by FBI agents on July 22, 1934. He had been given up by Anna Sage, "the Lady in Red," who, despite an agreement with the feds, was deported back to her native Romania. The Biograph was playing Manhattan Melodrama on that night.*

◄ **Ann Sather's Restaurant:** *This restaurant produces the creamiest, stickiest cinnamon rolls in Chicago, together with a menu of extraordinary Swedish "home-cooking." Ann Sather, a native Swede, opened her restaurant in 1945, on Belmont Avenue, later expanding to the Andersonville neighborhood which has a large Scandinavian population.*

▶ **The Second City:** *Founded in Chicago in 1959 as an improvisational comedy troop, The Second City has gone on to almost re-invent comedy in America. With many Second City alumni achieving critical success and with touring companies nationwide, it still presents cutting edge shows on their North Wells Street stage.*

Lincoln Square: *Sitting at the top of Lincoln Avenue, Lincoln Square was an ancestral homeland to Chicagoans of German heritage for many decades. Along the corridor of Lincoln Avenue, German restaurants provided a cuisine of remarkable authenticity.*

Though few "old world" Germans live there today, Lincoln Square still hosts an exciting outdoor Oktoberfest in this neighborhood that has been reborn and re-gentrified.

Steppenwolf Theatre: *Established in 1974 in a north suburban church basement, this is Chicago's premier theater company. Since it opened, actors like Gary Sinise, John Mahoney, John Malkovich, Laurie Metcalfe, and others have become well-known for*

their edgy, American stage productions, now in a state-of-the-art theater center on North Halstead Street.

▲ **Old Town:** *This is a piece of authentic Chicago neighborhood bordered by Division, LaSalle, Armitage, and Halsted Streets, and was largely settled as early as the 1850s by German immigrants. The area grew rapidly after the Great Fire. Legend has it that you can say you live in "Old Town" if you can hear the bells of St. Michael's Church, on Hudson Street, ring.*

The South Side

The city's South Side begins at Madison Street and is a vast expanse of urban landscape, dramatically larger than its North Side counterpart. The South Side is the area in which the Irish canal diggers settled, making a home where the waterway ended in a place known as Bridgeport. This small enclave has given the city five of its most enduring mayors—Kelly, Kennelly, Daley, Bilandic, and Daley. But the neighborhood was not only filled with Irish settlers. Italians, Croatians, Poles, and Lithuanians all settled here too and found employment alongside the Irish locals at the nearby Union Stockyards.

The area's most famous residents are the Chicago White Sox, who have made their home on 35th Street for almost a century. Charlie Comiskey, their founder, established the team here confident that the hard-working South Siders would never abandon the team. He was right.

When African-American inhabitants in the south responded to the challenge of *Chicago Defender* publisher Robert S. Abbott and began to leave Dixie for opportunities in the north during World War I, more than 100,000 people made what is referred to as the Great Migration. The South Side's Bronzeville became their historic home.

Mansions filled the streets of Kenwood and Hyde Park along the lake, several by the renowned Chicago architect Frank Lloyd Wright. In the late nineteenth century John D. Rockefeller endowed a university nearby with Standard Oil money, but humbly kept his name off the door. The University of Chicago is the Oxford of the Midwest, occupying an elegant ivy covered campus. The World's Columbian Exposition of 1893 was held in nearby Jackson Park: the Museum of Science and Industry is the only structure to remain after the Fair's closing. The U-505, the only German submarine to be captured on the high seas during World War II, is among its most enduring attractions. Local residents, at one time, included trust fund murderers Nathan Leopold and Richard Loeb who committed "the crime of the century." During World War II, Enrico Fermi split the atom in a University of Chicago lab. British sculpture Henry Moore created a monument that sits on the spot. It is said that snow never settles around the spot of the first sustained nuclear reaction. Modern architect Mies van der Rohe also chose to make the Illinois Institute of Technology his home and redesigned Chicago in his crisp style of glass and steel.

The South Side is the ancestral home of Chicago's endemic sense of bravado and unaffected attitude. It is the hothouse of local custom and unabashed prairie provincialism.

▶ **Midway Plaisance Park:** *This long sweeping parkway— one mile long and 300 feet wide—runs next to the medieval ivy-covered towers of the University of Chicago. In 1893 this "midway" was the heart of the World's Columbian Exposition's amusement park in which visitors rode the great revolving wheel by Ferris, and saw an Irish Village and a part of Cairo reconstructed.*

◄ **Museum of Science and Industry:** *This museum is one of the city's most popular attractions thanks to exhibits like the coal mine, the Apollo 8 spacecraft, and the U-505—the only German submarine to be captured on the high seas. The classically designed shell of the building was the only surviving structure from the 1893 World's Columbian Exposition, though it required almost total reconstruction to be made permanent.*

▶ **Chinatown:** *Now settled in the area of Cermak Road (22nd Street) and Wentworth Avenue, Chinatown was largely relocated there from the South Loop around 1912. The original community was inherently male due to the exclusionary laws prohibiting the immigration of Chinese women. Amid its colorful pagoda roofs and ancient archways, Chicago's Chinatown is a sea of fine restaurants, shops, and new homes, as well as a tightly connected community of local businesses.*

▶ **Jimmy's Woodlawn Tap:** *To be found at 1172 East 55th Street, Jimmy's Woodlawn Tap has been an important part of student life at the University of Chicago for more than 50 years. Here, collegiate brainiacs mix with blue-collar workers and urban professionals.*

◄ **DuSable Museum of African-American History:** *Originally opened in 1961 as The Ebony Museum of Negro History and Art, it was renamed in 1968 and became the DuSable Museum of African-American History, in honor of Chicago's first permanent settler, an Afro-Haitian fur trapper named Jean-Baptiste Point du Sable. For more than 40 years the museum has been collecting and preserving the heritage of African-Americans in Chicago.*

▶ **Oriental Institute:**
*This is among one of the
nation's more secretive
institutions. The collection
contains some of the most
extraordinary artifacts and
treasures of the ancient world
on earth. There are galleries
devoted to Egypt, Assyria,
Mesopotamia, Persia, and
Palestine. Among its prized
possessions is a fourteenth-
century B.C. 17-foot-tall
statue of King Tutankhamen.
This is "Indiana Jones" land.*

◀ **Mexican Fine Arts
Center Museum:** *The
artistic and cultural expression
of Chicago's dynamic Mexican
community is displayed with
power and panache within
the Mexican Fine Arts Center
Museum. The building was
originally designed by William
Carbys Zimmerman, an
Chicago architect in the firm
of Burnham and Root.*

▶ ▶ **Robie House:** *Near
the University of Chicago in
Hyde Park, at 5757 South
Woodlawn, is Frank Lloyd
Wright's most distinctive, and
well-known, domestic design.
Wright brought the Prairie-
style house to a new level of
elegance with the Robie
House, built in 1909. Utilizing
thin narrow Roman bricks and
sweeping cantilevered
horizontal roofs, Wright
expanded his use of "open
interior space," while at the
same time producing all of
the furniture, carpets, light
fixtures, and appliances.*

◀ **Richard J. Daley House:** *Nestled in the heart of the Bridgeport neighborhood, the Richard J. Daley Home, at 3536 South Lowe Avenue, displays the handsome, but modest, character of the "Chicago-style" bungalow. The Chicago Mayor spent his entire life in this Irish-Catholic working-class enclave that gave the city four other larger-than-life mayors, including his son.*

▶ **John J. Glessner House:** *This house, at 18th Street and Prairie Avenue, is a remarkable residence designed by Boston architect H. H. Richardson for the wealthy Glessners in 1887, on a street that was known as Chicago's "Millionaires Row." Fashioned in the Neo-Romanesque style, Glessner's granite mansion was a wonder of modern urban civility and intelligent reserve. Its modernity is said to have annoyed his neighbors. Now open to the public, it is an historic slice of Chicago life.*

▶ **U.S. Cellular Field:** *The home of the Chicago White Sox, the city's American League team, is at 333 West 35th Street. For generations, they played across the street in the stadium Charles Comiskey built back in 1914, known reverently as Comiskey Park. New owners razed the old park in the early 1990s and fashioned this new post-modern stadium.*

◀ **Union Stockyards:**
*Opened on Christmas Day
1865, the Union Stockyards,
on 43rd and Halsted, was
responsible for helping to
make Chicago the commercial
capital of the nation. Over the
ensuing century, Chicago
meatpackers like Swift,
Armour, and Morris changed
the way Americans ate by
shipping their dressed meats
via refrigerated railcars coast
to coast. The stockyards were
closed in 1971 and all that
remains are the entrance
gates of Illinois limestone.*

▶ **Schaller's Pump:** *This
Bridgeport neighborhood, at
37th and Halsted Streets, is
located directly across the
street from the 11th Ward
Regular Democratic
Organization, the political
domain of the late Mayor
Richard J. Daley. Schaller's
served Chicago's best Butt
Steak Sandwich and Hash-
browned potatoes. It is a local
institution.*

◀ **South Kenwood
Mansions:** *This is the
neighborhood directly south of
Hyde Park. During the last
decades of the nineteenth
century it was a luxurious
community of stately
mansions built by the city's
most successful barons. Frank
Lloyd Wright left his imprint
here, as did the city's finest
architects. After decades of
neglect, this neighborhood was
revitalized and once more
shimmers in its own beauty.*

◀ **University of Chicago:** *The university is one of America's most prestigious academic institutions. Founded in 1892, when John D. Rockefeller provided it with initial funding, he insisted that the school would not bear his name, though its nearby resplendent chapel does. Modeled on the great universities of Germany, today its graduate students far outnumber its undergrads. During World War II, scientists here split the atom. There are more Nobel Prize recipients here than at any other institution in the world.*

▶ **South Shore Cultural Center:** *Originally built as South Shore Country Club, in 1906, South Shore Cultural Center, at 71st Street and South Shore Drive, sits alongside the waters of Lake Michigan in an affluent neighborhood of grand balls and high social life. When urban transition changed neighborhood life, the club was purchased by the Chicago Park District in 1972 and is maintained as the jewel in its lakefront crown.*

Pullman: The area on Chicago's far south side, at 111th Street, was originally an experimental company town built in the early 1880s for workers in George Pullman's railcar construction industry. Pullman's stranglehold on resident workers was legendary and later became the cause of one of the city's greatest labor battles. It was an experiment run amok, but today the architectural legacy of the town remains rich and long-lasting.

Original Rainbow Cone: Chicago's famous ice cream parlor can be found at 9233 South Western Avenue, in the Beverly neighborhood. It has been creating extravagant cones sine 1926 and is a south side way-of-life in summer. With layers of chocolate, strawberry, pistachio, and cherry ice cream, together with orange sherbet, Rainbow has been pleasing locals for decades.

Washington Park: Laid out in 1873 by the great landscape architect Frederick Law Olmstead 'the father of American landscape architecture', who created Central Park in New York, today the park is the venue for countless urban programs and festivals.

▲ **Chicago Skyway:** *Built by the city in 1958, the Chicago Skyway is a 7.8-mile toll roadway. Erected in an era when super-highway construction was just beginning and transforming American life, the toll plaza reflects the Mid-Century Modern architectural design of* *the period and burnished stainless steel toll booths that have a unique "space-age" feel to them. Leased for 99 years to a European consortium for $1.82 billion, Chicago no longer operates the skyway, America's first privatized roadway.*

▶ **Pilsen Neighborhood's Murals:** *These murals are a dramatic urban art form reflective of the rich Mexican cultural character of this neighborhood, once home to Bohemian and Czech immigrants in another century. They display the intimate details of urban life here in a* *community re-gentrifying, yet trying to maintain its traditions.*

▶ **Illinois Institute of Technology:** *The institute, on 3300 South State Street, was home to the great Mies van der Rohe, the city's most dynamic modern architect. He has left his imprint everywhere, especially in the low-rise modernity of the campus buildings he designed. In the twenty-first century, those he influenced have brought their own fresh designs to the campus. The McCormick Tribune Campus Center by Rem Koolhaas, features a titanium tube through which the nearby "EL" passes, diminishing its noise. Helmut Jahn's State Street Village student resident hall has a 550-foot long curving stainless steel exterior. Architecture is king here.*

◀ **Chicago Daily Defender Building:** *The newspaper's headquarters on South Michigan Avenue was once a showroom palace in what is known as "Motor Row." Founded by publisher Robert S. Abbott in 1905, the newspaper has been called "the mouthpiece of 14 million people." Abbott challenged the African-Americans in the south to leave the land of oppression and come to northern cities like Chicago during World War I. The Great Migration brought 100,000 people to Chicago. The paper has been a catalyst for civil and human rights in America since its establishment.*

▶ **K.A.M. Isaiah Israel Temple:** *K.A.M. is the city's oldest Jewish Congregation. Organized in 1847, it built its first synagogue in Chicago in 1851. Later, locating to 33rd and Indiana, in a building designed by Adler and Sullivan (Adler's father was the rabbi), the congregation merged with the Isaiah Israel Congregation. Today the community is based in this remarkable Byzantine building in Hyde Park.*

▶ **Willie Dixon's Blues Heaven Foundation:** *This is an important arts-based philanthropic organization housed in the landmark "Chess Record Studio," at 2120 South Michigan Avenue. Blues legend Willie Dixie founded the group in 1970 to help stabilize the lives of blues and jazz musicians.*

Index

Map of Chicago

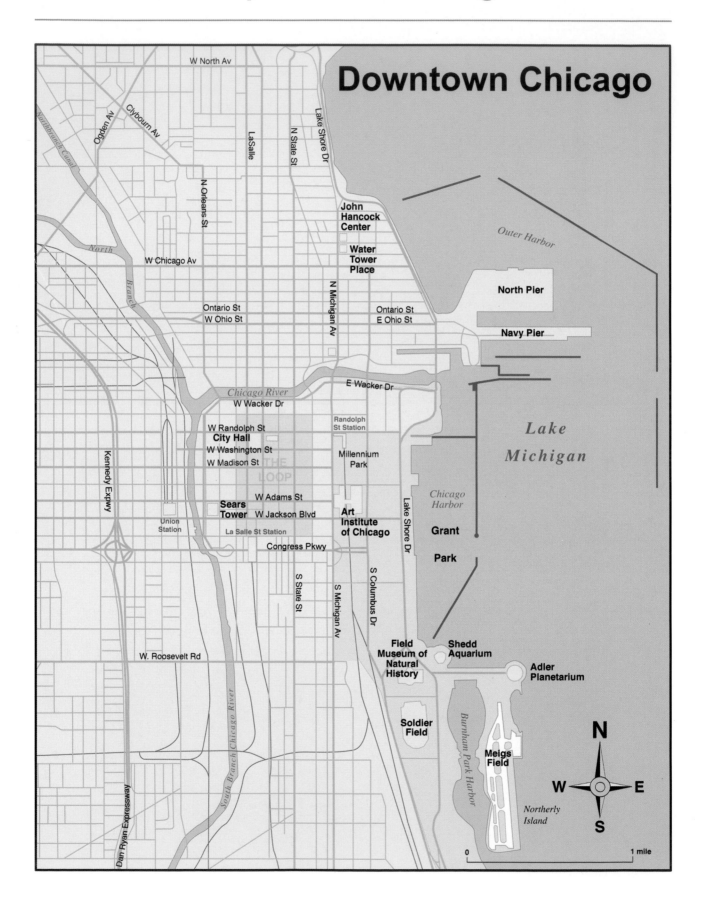

Downtown Chicago

W North Av

Outer Harbor

Ogden Av

Clybourn Av

Northbranch Canal

LaSalle

N Orleans St

N State St

Lake Shore Dr

North

Branch

W Chicago Av

John Hancock Center

Water Tower Place

North Pier

Ontario St
W Ohio St

N Michigan Av

Ontario St
E Ohio St

Navy Pier

E Wacker Dr

Chicago River
W Wacker Dr

W Randolph St
City Hall
W Washington St
W Madison St

THE LOOP

Randolph St Station

Millennium Park

Lake Michigan

Kennedy Expwy

Chicago Harbor

W Adams St
Sears Tower   W Jackson Blvd

Union Station

La Salle St Station

Art Institute of Chicago

Lake Shore Dr

Grant

Park

Congress Pkwy

S State St

S Michigan Av

S Columbus Dr

W. Roosevelt Rd

Field Museum of Natural History

Shedd Aquarium

Adler Planetarium

South Branch Chicago River

Burnham Park Harbor

Soldier Field

Meigs Field

Dan Ryan Expressway

Northerly Island

N

W   E

S

0   1 mile